Shevaun Cooley | Homing

New Poems

GIRAMONDO POETS

Shevaun Cooley

Homing

First published 2017
from the Writing & Society Research Centre
at the University of Western Sydney
by the Giramondo Publishing Company
PO Box 752 Artarmon NSW 1570 Australia
www.giramondopublishing.com

Designed by Harry Williamson
Typeset by Andrew Davies
in 10/16.5 pt Baskerville BT

Printed and bound by Ligare
Distributed in Australia by NewSouth Books

National Library of Australia
Cataloguing-in-Publication data:

Cooley, Shevaun –
Homing / Shevaun Cooley
ISBN 978-1-925336-20-7 (pbk)

A821.4

for everyone still trying to make their way home

Acknowledgements

Poems from this collection have appeared in the following publications: *Cordite*, *Dazzled: the University of Canberra Vice-Chancellor's International Poetry Prize Anthology*, *The Fremantle Press Anthology of Western Australian Poetry*, *Meanjin* and *Southerly*. My thanks to the editors.

Dr Marcella Polain has offered unwavering support and a perceptive critical eye. She is the kindest advocate I could have wished for myself and my work. These poems formed part of my doctoral work at Edith Cowan University; for their feedback, my sincere thanks to Dr Ffion Murphy and Associate Professor Susan Ash at ECU, and to Judith Beveridge and Philip Gross. Fellow poets Matt Roberts and Nandi Chinna gave utterly honest and always good-humoured feedback in the tiniest of poetry groups. I wrote many of the 'Welsh' poems in the cottage, Glan-y-Don; thanks to Richard Baxter for his generosity. For their hard work and more, my thanks to Fiona Wright, Ivor Indyk and the team at Giramondo. Lastly, to my family and friends – too many to mention – my infinite love and gratitude.

Contents

34°24'13.6"S 115°11'43.9"E

37 every night is a rinsing myself of the darkness

38 not like me whose migrations are endless

Grain, Ground, Grasp: Three Ghazals

45 the true trade: to go with the grain

47 it was I it ground

48 there are no handrails to grasp

52°45'34.4"N 4°47'11.6"W

53 deep down is as distant as far out, but is arrived at in no time

55 worse things: our shadows, for instance

57 in the hushed meadows the weasel

58 meadows empty of him, animal eyes, impersonal as glass

61 who, blind, saw
63 the line trembles; mostly, when we would
reel in the catch, there is nothing to see
68 about mountains it is useless to argue,
70 an absence is how we become surer of what
72 I was no tree walking
77 like an old tree lightened of the
snow's weight
79 we have eaten the blackberries and spat
out the seeds, but they lie glittering like
the eyes of a man
82 ran with a dark current
84 trees are about you
88 I have no name for today but itself
90 the stars are fixed, but the earth journeys
by strange migrations towards the cold
93 all those good words; and I outside them
96 I hid myself in the side of the mountain

34°24’13.6”S

115°11’43.9”E

without catching a thing I was not far from the truth

an Easter road trip

If I closed my eyes for a minute
I would be lost, yet
I could gladly lie down and sleep forever
beside this road. RAYMOND CARVER

Spy Wednesday

1

We cross the bridge over Poison Gully.
Nothing happens, or has yet happened.

2

L. asks if I write poems for my friends.
He's thinking of himself. Never, I say.
It occurs to me that this is a lie.
Of course I write poems for dead
friends. This seems now to be some kind
of terrible error.

3 *Corrigin*

There's no sign anymore of the burning.
The land has grown used to it, even if
we have not. Do you want to stop,
says L. I don't. We are as soon
out of the town as we were in it.

I won't be carrying on about death.
Some things you shouldn't use up,
even if you want to. How did she die,
asks L. and I tell him: in a bushfire.
That's a horrible way to die, he says.

Before us, on the road, the centre line
begins to split, lit up by our passing.

Maundy Thursday

1

They say Easter is a moveable
feast. Does that mean it can
be carried like us at speed,
the fields rushing by on
both sides, emptied
of grain?

2

At last at Lucky Bay, we swim, though dusk
is coming on. On the shore, in the decayed seaweed,
a young kangaroo gnaws on something. We close
in on it. It's not afraid of us. That's a dead fish, I say.
It is stiff in the roo's paws, hardened to petrifaction.

Later the ranger says, we have no idea why
they eat what they eat. They're scavengers.
After dark, I'll see one licking a tray of meat drippings

at the base of the barbecue. None of this seems
right, I want to say. But there is no one close to
offer a reply.

3

L. says if you put it to your ear
you might hear the sand break
in your hand. Underfoot, it cries
out as we walk, so fine we
have a hard time washing
the grains from our feet.

Good Friday

I *Frenchman's Peak*

It's said the flat rocks in the bay's shallows
are the bodies of two children who dared

to steal the eagle's eggs. She plucked up
the children and dropped them in the deeps;

and each time they made for shore she took
them again, dropped them again, kept on at it

until the children faltered and died. It's said
the mother eagle still keeps watch that they not

dare to rise. We walk her steep flank.
At the peak, a great hooded arch of rock –
an eye that can't close.

2

It's also said the arch was made by the repeated
breaking of waves against it, back when the sea
was two hundred metres higher.

The French who made landfall here named
this place 'Hope'. For a moment I see how
we're walking under water.

3 *Lucky Bay*

We try fishing from the rocks.
There's a surging tide, barely
any light. L. casts twice

but the rigging catches
again and again. I take a turn,
cast out, and see the float

glow in an arc over the darkening
sea. There's a curious sense
of lightness, but it is only

because I've somehow
broken the line.

Holy Saturday

I

Back to driving this road. It is dead
straight, but undulating. Ahead

the bitumen is interrupted
by patches of uncorrupted light.

Brief moments when we're caught
in the light, then as quickly, we're out

of it. We pass more dead kangaroos.
Two dead parrots, a decomposed fox,

the striated ribs of a carcass picked clean.
South of here, the rabbit-proof fence leans

tiredly into the sea. It has come a long way.
When it comes down to it, I might only

write poems when I can feel how death
rides the edges. It's the car that travels

in your blind spot, the roadkill pressed
into the road's shoulder, rotting to the gravel.

2

I once spent a Holy Saturday on the island of Paros.
While we ate dinner by the quietening Aegean, a man
strode past us with a flayed lamb on his shoulder. Later,
my friend walked past the kitchen, where the same man worked

with a large butcher's machete, precise, almost delicate,
severing the limbs, the lolling head. When we say *sacrilegious*
we mean someone has stolen a sacred thing. But not that loose
tongue, those once-agile hooves, or even the light in the eye.

Easter Sunday

I *Gibraltar Rock, Porongurup Ranges*

L. looks up at the dome of rock,
then further up to the clear sky.
We should turn back, he says,

it looks like a storm coming in –
I know you're scared of lightning.
I don't look at him. Just tie in, I say.

By the end of the day our palms
will be almost raw. This kind of climbing
asks that you press the rock

with the heels of your hands
and then step cautiously up on tiny
footholds. 240 metres of it; granite

worn by 1100 million years
of weather. You think you're
worn out, I'd like to say.

I take in the last of the rope
and L. pulls himself into the cave
at the top of the second pitch.

I hate you, he says.
We peel and eat boiled eggs.
We share an orange.

It's already mid-afternoon,
the distant range of the
Stirlings hazy. I get back to it,

make the hardest move
out of the cave. We are not
even halfway there.

Eleven hundred million years.
L. shows me a wound on his hand.
It weeps a little.

2 *Night reading in the Porongurups*
The Egyptians believed
they descended from the tears

of the sun, who created the Earth,
and then wept at its beauty.

And the tears turned the earth
to mud and the mud became the first

of us. The Sumerians believed
they came from the clay. But we're

not so interested in origins today.
Earlier, in the camp kitchen two men

gutted fish on the sink. They said,
at Nanarup today the salmon ran in such

numbers, they could feel the fish collide
with their submerged legs.

Easter Monday

1

We cross the bridge over Fifty–Two Creek.
I have all kinds of questions.

2

I tell him I am writing a poem called
Ten Arguments With L. and
that each will end with the line
and L. lost the argument. He says,

but I never do. I say, of course you
do. And yes, L. loses the argument.

3
Can I say this now?
This is a poem
for you all, my
friends, not
because you will
die, or have died
but because you live
so miraculously
well.

4 *Near Kojonup*
The traffic is slow, an endless line.
We're descending, when a car
ascending the next hill veers
to the right, across the lane, stirs up

a brief plume of gravel dust, then over-
corrects, cutting back to our side of the road.
It disappears somewhere off to the left.
There's more dust, maybe smoke.

I can still see the curve it inscribed
across the highway. We don't say
a thing. And because the traffic is slow,
and slowing more,

it takes some time before
we pull near enough to see for ourselves
whether, in the end, he saved himself
or not.

call your horizons in

Hard as an icon, the sky,
and almost as untouchable. In Flinders Bay,
the sea is only partway through its sweeping. A perigean tide

as high as you've ever seen begins now to ebb, an unseasonal creep
that draws away the white sand, leaves the dark
mineral glitter

of ilmenite. They say the grains
are faintly magnetic. Is that why you put your hands
to it? Get off your knees. They say the water is never warm like

this unless a current runs from the north, dragging the sea-
bed, unsettling whatever is used to sinking in.
That must be why you're in it

to your ankles. When the white-
headed petrel lifts itself from the shore
you can watch it all you like, but it brings nothing

closer. If you could ride with it, would you gather in the end-
lessness, or wheel your hunting down to the silver
flash of a fin?

You've quickened
now to the blunt horizon. The seaweed

has a hayricked, iodine stink. Dead inkfish line the shore,
their Rorschach bodies a clue to what stops the pulse. I said get of
your knees. Let's see what the petrel draws in
with its cry.

the bone the island

11th February, 1945, 10:15pm: 11 miles due south of Cape Leeuwin, N Class Destroyer HMAS Nizam *was hit broadside by a large wave. Ten men were swept overboard, and never found.*

1

as when the meal is done and between
one sentence and the next you turn
and scrape away the leftovers

what was I saying, you say

2

One wave is like another
until it is not; and men
asleep on deck are
lifted off asleep

and closed into the fist
of the wave

and then the list
is righted

and far below, one
of them – it might

be the youngest – tries
to say deep in the
draughting down:

I disagree

3

[etymology]
seel: to roll as a ship at sea

: to close the eyes of a hawk
with thread drawn through
the lids, then fastened
over the head

4

Able Seaman Allen Wilfred Milich
10th February 1945
To his brother Min:

It's as cold as buggary where
we are, when we go on
watch we are dressed like
Russian ski troopers; if we fell
overboard we'd go straight
to the bottom,
I'm sure

(but, brother what if
this gullying downward is not
death. What if we
are the nothing that happened and keeps
happening.
I am
a something I don't
even
think

the unfathomable hundred
needles behind the eye

the thousand cicadas
of the ear
bursting out
of life)

5

[etymology]
heel: to lean to one
side *especially of a boat*
or ship

: either of the projections
of a coffin bone *&* **:** a bone
of the foot below the ankle &

: part of the palm of the hand
nearest the wrist

6

as when the albatross takes up the ballast
stone and heaves it downward to break open
a hard mollusc; then plucks up the stone
and begins again

it can't cry with a stone in its mouth
it will do this until the light dies

there is an island there is no going to

looking out to St Alouarn's Island

It's like this – well before
dusk, but the sun long gone
behind the western hills. Whatever
the wind is up to, it's somehow
winnowing the light to the edges
of the high cirrus.

I mean – a wingspan of darkness has come in
over this corner of land. But the island stays alight, out
to the south-east. A deep-buried ember that never gutters entirely,
it flares up like the bronchial longing I can't shift
from my chest.

It means – it's maybe a curse. *Island's full*
of rabbits and snakes, old Sam Griffith said, when I asked
what he'd found there. *It's too hard to make landfall.*
You have to go to the side you've never seen. It's best in a flat-
bottomed scow, but no one can make the crossing
in one of those.

It was simple for Louis de St Alouarn. A sea-sick man
falls where he lands, flaking out the rope of himself over whatever
stands still. But what stands, still, over there?
And what is a metaphor for, if it can't carry us
across the simplest of marine distances.

In what is hardly left of the afternoon,
the terns wallow and cry with some preternatural
bitterness. They're not landlocked, but they say it
anyway: *cur cur cur-r-r...*stuttering out a word
they don't dare finish.

I mean – those are welts in the sky.
I mean to stand still and wait for the island
to lift from its smoulder. For the tern to
turn towards me, and see for myself
the darker trailing edge
of its underwing.

word only becomes at last the word

At the foot of Bluff Knoll, a man forgets the word
for his knees. He stops, wildered. Aren't there currents
everywhere that might snag us? Those clouds

holding the peak are how Noatch comes down
from wherever she hides, so lonely she can't keep her form
for long. She mourns like vapour, and will drag you to the ground.

The mountain is a cresting wave distracted from its motion.
On the peak, wind caught hold of the plastic wrap
of my sandwich, snatched it from the bluff.

Thermal-lifted, almost-bodied. Two swallows launched
at it from the cliff and harried it away, as if it were
a strange, transparent bird, or else loneliness again

grasping for shape. The three of them swept and receded
toward Toolbrunup and Mt Trio, where at the base,
someone was doing a controlled burn, and vanished

into the afternoon glare and smoke haze.
Dead body spirit. Those clouds in the retina.
Knees, I say at last. Knees.

I spelled out the word 'lonely'.
And my hand moved to erase it: but
I'm as lonely as … as Franz Kafka. FRANZ KAFKA

There was no storm. But where the nets had been,
they found only unbrushed
water, silent weed
in the depths. They call them

ghost nets, those torn and let drift
on the tides. Or like my father's net, found stripped

on a wind-raw beach, driven into shore by
the dumping waves, and rolled, unlike
any sleeping thing, into
a sand-heavy bundle.

I've had dreams too, Kafka.
How we always run, you and I, with treacle

at our feet. Is it loneliness you'd call it,
to watch those men mend the shredded
net outside my uncle's shed, how
they cradled it

in their laps, how I held my own
cut sandwich, uneaten, how

the net needles clicked,
steady as metronomes,

that keep time, but do not seem, like you
or I, marked by its passing?

Soundings

In the winter of 1986, 114 false killer whales were stranded on a beach in Flinders Bay, Western Australia

1

The bends: [n] Nautical. *The wales of a vessel. Things of bent shape. Or, decompression sickness.*

To be the first of them:
coming up from the twilit plain,
upswelling to the shallows – the draft
of your keel growing less; to rise

though you don't yet
know why, hauling in on the bitter
end until you hit air hard as granite,
the concrete winter light;

to be beneaped then, and bent;
for the first time to feel the utter weight
of yourself – enough, if you don't retreat,
to shatter you.

2

What floats after *falling* is
flotsam, and what floats when *thrown* is *jetsam*.
Whatever sinks is *lagan*.

3

Whatever is cast up
is *ours*.

stone: [v] . To scrub lecks with , so called the work e done on e's knees.)

4

And we threw over their fretting skin
sea-wetted hessian and kept on with the wetting

the whole body a fever under
our hands.

yal zone: om Greek ýs), deep. *f 1000 to tres below n surface.* ght zone)

5

Like the sentence
you didn't see coming

they rise up wrecked before
you and you think it is not that they're
like electricity suddenly here

it's that somehow they were always
already out there.

6

; or, The Whale

All men live enveloped
in whale-lines.

7

(soundings: [n] archaic. *The area of sea close to the shore, shallow enough for the bottom to be reached by means of a sounding line. Or, a logbook of these particulars.)*

To be the first of them:
coming over the dunes,
the spinifex bending and unbending

the dog keening hard out on the leash

and out to the south the long sea
grey under the cloud-linger;

to cast your eyes down
and see them lined up, blackly
magnificent, the hundred in the sharp
air dying

to hear them sigh against the wave;
to be the first to move to
salvage them.

it is not the river carrying us away

The armoured bream glint
and scatter. We bunt the hull
against a submerged pylon. The anchor
chatters its chain against the gunwale and
vanishes. We can feel in the swing of the dinghy
how the anchor kites in dark silt thin
almost as the water itself.

This is how the river catches:
hauling what it can from underfed creeks,
widening to pools where the tiger snake,
quick as history, swims in patches
of water warmed to a green
opacity. How many spirits
are caught in the phosphate
run-off, tugged, almost weightless,
against underwater rocks, torn at times,
only to come back together?

Rivers are secretive. They do something
to time. But only rarely do they catch fire –
the day smoking down on us, the cold cinder
crumble of a paperbark under hand, the hot sheet
of the surface at sunset, the hook in the eye
of a whiting. When the anchor is raised,
it's a dead weight, laden flukes trailing dark

mud as it emerges. We have caught
almost nothing. But we hear,
in the beginnings of night
how, on the river, even
a voice is ash,
at last hushed.

I have let her ashes down in me like an anchor

Now you barely open
your eyes. Your hands thinner
than the afternoon shadow.

We were once on our knees
in the wet edges of the shore.
Not praying, but attending to
dozens of stranded false killer
whales, lined like dark body
bags on the long stretch
of beach.

Your father used to light
lamps on the bridges over the Swan River,
whistling quietly as he set the wicks
to burning. Even then, they used
natural gas.

We had forgotten
almost entirely how the bodies
we soothed to stillness on the shore
held a secret of
combustibility –

And they didn't burn, or light up
our tired faces, but were ushered
back out to sea.

I will slip through the eye of the needle on which the saved are to be threaded

If we are in motion are we more,
or less, real? There's no-one to tell us

if these are the right questions. We try
an experiment at three thousand feet,

fly the Saratoga at a *cumulus mediocris*,
to know at last if we will drill through,

or break apart the cloud, or if it will close
again behind us, unruffled.

This cloud becomes an unforgiving wall
we pitch ourselves at. Is it the smallest

of miracles that we pass through?
Is all of the sky at last ours?

What are clouds but particles lifted, gathered?
Warmed to the visible, like words.

Kite-surfers ellipse on the river below.
And the river, which has its own thoughts,

turns against the banks, snakes more
and more toward the Dead Water.

At least one shag on a post shakes
its wings to dry in the salted light.

The sky's not really the limit of anything.
Now we know it, the corner of infinity lifted.

We turn back on ourselves, bank south, then east.
The cloud is halved, or doubled. More, then

or less, desolate?

let down at birth into the dark well and overflowing with it

Wednesday's Child

is that what you think
poet, what do they mean full of
woe, are we receptacles always
learning the best way
to contain

Celan never quite said *keep yes*
and no unspilt, dark wells we,
with answers cupped
in the palms, so full
they fall through
our fingers

once we'd have said over
the last sheaf, *Wodan*
gallops across:
the harvest done,
Wednesday's god rode
his white horse
through stubble,
collecting the cut
souls, driving them
out

clearing
the shed, my father
found a rusted scythe,
perfectly crafted, it was
possible just in the holding
to imagine the motion
it asked for, its use locked
into its form, the un-
splintered grips,
the curve of the snath

I stood on the already-
mowed grass and reaped
the air, cut swathes
you'd never see,
the light suddenly clear
as if an old cry
whyed tautly
across the low hills
and west to the sea

is there a leak somewhere in the mind

He and I walk the riverbank. An egret scuds the water, stiff-legge
as if tied at its thin ankles. I know nothing of what the egret feels:
the opening of its wings, the lift, to be always light in the bones.
Our hands are cold. Or mine are. I won't ask about his hands.

An egret is only a bird. It pierces the shallows of its own
reflection, breaks the calm into concentric circles.
Egress is when a planet emerges from an eclipse. Or what
happens when you make a break for it. How the plates of the eart

shift and soil turns to liquid and gouts up. It's the way signals seep
into one another. He showed me once how to design a dam; he kne
how best to stop a leak. What are his hands doing today, then.
The egret flees us, upriver. Regret is something else altogether.

where to turn without turning to stone

Some days I have nothing left but to lean
over the smallest plants, to see
if they have yet grown.
I love most
the succulents; those
that will take root from a fallen leaf,
then let the leaf wither as if it never mattered.

Some nights I'm afraid I might wake
to find my jaw hinged open.
Like Celan, maybe; who
once walked
Boulevard Saint-Michel shedding
the unwanted pages of the weekend
Die Zeit until it could fold in his pocket, then

caught a bus across the Seine, and alighted
to find the newspaper again complete
at his feet. *This happens to me*
with everything, every
day, he said. It's good to know
a curse when you see it. To know at least
that it will always return entire. It didn't matter

that Celan altered his name, or became a stone
to break through the grey Seine. On days

when I have nothing left,
I lower myself
even nearer the earth. I show
my friend the fallow plot. What do I do
with this, I ask. What you always
do, she says.
Use it.

every night is a rinsing myself of the darkness

[*Lucian Freud,* Naked man with Rat, *1977/78*]

Each dusk the same – a billow of its sails
presses the dark hard against the skylight.
You wake with the furies in your chest.
Perhaps the severed tail of a pale skink,
its twitch underfoot, fierce and lifeless,
was not a dream. Still, the feel of it rides

in the *no* in your throat, the luminosity
of your blood that wells up to the skin
without breaking. You want to be held
without being touched – the air bright
around you with the hope of it. At last,
it seems something lowers itself in order

to see you. You don't move, but sense its trace,
so light and exquisite, at rest on your upper thigh.

not like me whose migrations are endless

During this storme certain great fowles as big as swannes, soared about us … and from the poynt of one wing to the poynt of the other, both stretched out, was about two fathoms.
RICHARD HAWKINS

1

The albatross is a ship.
It might founder into the sea
for want of wind. The albatross knows

lack is the heaviest thing of all.

To shipwreck an albatross,
make it land on water, then take
the wind out

of its sails.

2

Now I am ready to tell how bodies are changed
into different bodies.

Remember Acmon of Pleuron
was turned to a bird
throat-first, his voice thinning,
narrowed of neck.
As Ovid tells it,

the man became plumed
and feathered and bent.
His elbows cambered to wing.
It was big-mouthed Acmon who,
when all seemed lost, goaded Venus,
said, *what else have you got,*
and then he got it, big mouth
hardened
to a beak.

Remember Lycus,
who gaped in amazement,
then too transformed; and Rhexener
and Nycteus
and Idas and Abas;
who when they lifted
to the sky could not bring
themselves yet to wheel
away from their own ship
and cried above it. These men,
let's be precise, whose bodies
were very nearly, but not quite,
like those of snowy swans.

Remember Diomede, who they say at last
joined his men, but only after long
years of grief; who could not
aid those who asked for it,

because he had no men
to offer.
They had winged away.
Men are albatross,
anyway.

3

The flood of 1982 washed the first
Alexander Bridge into the Blackwood,
its jarrah-trunk pylons river-rolled all
the way to the sea.

There is one half-buried
in the shore of Flinders Bay,
sand-logged but still whole.
It has drift in its core,

remembers how without wings
it rode a current.

4

At the sight
of the albatross,
the sailor Richard Hawkins
measured its wingspan
in fathoms.

5

After Baudelaire

The poet is some
storm-hunting bird,
who lords over clouds
and mocks the men who
point from below

but shackled now
to the heckling earth,
struggles to walk
for her giant
wings.

6

Tell me I'm done with
changing.

Grain, Ground, Grasp: Three Ghazals

the true trade: to go with the grain

When the Messiah comes and the world ends … those people
buried at the Mount of Olives ... will be first to awaken and
arise in paradise. Those people buried elsewhere on the planet,
tradition says, will 'roll through the earth' till they come up there.
ANNIE DILLARD

Cross the high *meseta* of central Spain in summer, and
you will see nothing
on either side but fields of wheat, the air's dry grain.

Under open skies in France, there was a time to declare *the wolf*
is passing through, at waves of wind flattening the grain: they knew

what it means to be unsettled. 'Paul Celan chews a word
like a stone,'
said Jean Daive. 'All day long. It produces word-energy.'
He could see it pulse

in the muscles of Celan's jaw. With enough pressure
even sand will turn to glass.
But even this begins with the simple matter of a few grains pressed

hard against each other. I wonder whether Sisyphus began to push
only a kernel of earth that grew as he rolled it uphill.
Would it be worse,

to see it grow? The weariness, when it comes these days, is sudden
and complete. As if we'd been working all this time
against the grain, or

turned the wrong way to stare at the sun; could see the surface
of it, where the plasma shifts and lifts in currents, a
photosphere of granules

no longer invisible to us. We rub our eyes raw, begin to let our skin
catch on the world. Who's to say what we'll find when
we emerge, dishevelled,
out of the earth?

it was I it ground

Ground, like sleep, forgets for a living. PHILIP GROSS

The horse, long-legged and dark, descends through the field.
You hear his approach. He drags up the thunder from the ground.

It's as if there are creatures you can dream into being,
a warrior emerging from the field of Ares, a rift of earth.

Those are phosphenes you see – symmetrical burning squares,
flashing grilles – when you grind your fists into your eyes.

Oubliette comes from the French word for *forgetting*,
since no one likes to remember a man left in the ground.

On the way to your grandmother's funeral, you held a can of tuna
uselessly in your hand. We take utmost care, it read, to pulverise

or remove them, but some bones may remain. Can you tell me
if *tribute* has anything to do with *tributary* – the underground

streams that feed a river, are they also gifts? I know an island
with no trees, unstoppable winds that leave potatoes unearthed.

In LAX, a man showed me a map. *This is the formidable desert,*
he said. *And I have no desire to cross that ground –*

not like you, who – coyly? coolly? – walk the edge of the field
not knowing what else will fall, or rise up, to break your thirst.

there are no handrails to grasp

And then, before the late supper, this pensiveness over the hands in the silver washbasin. Could any coherence be brought into what they did? any order or continuity in their grasping and releasing? No. All men attempted both the thing and its opposite. All men cancelled themselves out, there was no such thing as action. RAINER MARIA RILKE

All of these nights I spend now with an arm hooked
over a hard pillow, as if sleep will only happen if I hold

it down. Black birds wheel under the low-pressed palm of sky.
I want to know if *Ave Maria* might mean *Mary, the bird*, who grasps

at a sky she is also tumbling from. I walked by the lake
in the morning, and broke through the grip of ice at its edges

with the tip of a stick. I walked by the lake in the evening,
and it had healed over. The new ice was thin as comprehension,

more transparent than what surrounded it. In 1947,
in the rectory in Manafon, the poet R.S. Thomas was trapped

in a night of 23 degrees below, cold enough to brighten the stars.
'I was aware of the house cracking and grieving as the frost
            tightened

its grip,' he wrote. I've known nights like that, only it was my bones –
radius, ulna – that let out small noises of pressure and bare release.
I'm seized

too by inaction. Once the osprey has locked the spicules of its talons
on a fish, its grip ratchets further in and it cannot let go; we know

that at times the bird will drown before it has the chance to release
the thrashing fish in its grip. I dive, I dive. It's not a matter of
learning,

but a lack of some other instinct, Shevaun, that keeps you keeping.
Just as this is not diving, but catching at what swims furiously always
downward.

52°45’34.4”N

4°47’11.6”W

deep down is as distant as far out, but is arrived at in no time

1

To grieve what is not yet gone?
I have no word for that. Beneath the low
sky today, the river Glaslyn deepens
and greens. Moss seems to thicken
on the ground, the lichen-wracked boughs
of the oaks. A pair of simple ducks work
upstream. Their wake lifts the frost
on the banks. To the man who is

almost not here, grief is a claw.
It's how it sounds to his ear; a hover
of talons. The crows here, I've noticed,
cry three times, less gravel in their throats
than the birds I've known. They protest:
why, why and why.

2

I can't hear the rain, only see how it breaks
the river. In the kitchen, serving spoons
gleam on the wall. He's folding his jeans.
Is it possible that all streams that enter the river
might keep themselves for a time. For every
irrepressible thing, is something else
subsumed. The ground already waterlogged,
the frost gone.

The light is losing its grip on all but the tips
of Cnicht, Moelwyn Fawr and Fach. Until it
is only in the muted silver of the river,
which seems now without current, as if
its stillness was the trick
of holding.

worse things: our shadows, for instance

A Welsh Gothic

1

At the old farmhouse of Erwsuran, the ghosting
black tiger has long been banished to the black lake.
But the white tiger passes through the laundry,
pads the flagstones, brushes the still-damp piles
of sheets, leaves by the back door, and disappears
for a time over the Fedw scarp. In winter,
we have seen moss grow in her wet tracks.

2

I would like to shake the dream.
Always pregnant with twins, in
the tumbledown
shed, again
opening in the dim light
a sackful of dead white ferrets. Is it still my
task to skin them? Their eyes

the last pennies in the jar.

3

It's not the floods you should be fearing,
says Ianto, when the rains come. The river
rises behind him. In these parts, it's the things
the waters bring down. In the valley, wasn't a

woman clean killed in her kitchen by a stone?
Washed straight through the second-floor
window. The river rises behind his grin.

4

Sure, it's all unpredictable.
The old man at the bus stop
in Porthmadog, a goitre huge
under the jaw,
turns to me. We Welsh say
it's like the trees. You never know when
it's going to come down.

in the hushed meadows the weasel

Turned away from the sea, tired of the shifting
blues. I'd like to know what else there is. Please.
The days stretch out but the light seems to be closing
off, a hand on the shutter. At midday in the field,
I saw the weasel. The air suppled by her eager
spine, and in her paws rose the dusky scent

of damp earth and dung, of blood, a seed long
embedded. She was nothing at all; less
than a reddish passing, some deadly surprise
that sinuates sometimes through each of us.
I think now I have waited my whole life to pass
through a field of white flowers and long grass –

like that, light as a murderer. To be the small fire
that bursts the earth into being beneath, then dies.

meadows empty of him, animal eyes, impersonal as glass

Aubades

to be a part of the outward life, to be out there at the edge of things, to let the human taint wash away in emptiness and silence as the fox sloughs his smell in the cold unworldliness of water.

J.A. BAKER

I

There is the time before the knowing.
When I see the fox, and stop
my breath.
It is so light on the path –
there will be no pawprints in the hard
earth. Rain drifts
grainily in
the air, but I have felt nothing
on my skin for hours. It is the time, after
all, before the knowing,

which is not time, but the pausing of it.
It trots toward me, noses
the wet under-
brush, keeping to the edges
of the path, delicate as the breath not
taken, the unmoving

air, that must
have moved – since it starts,
and scents in me what I've not sensed,
the deepest predatory

wish; that I want only to pin it down, bury
my face in its winter fur.
Struck now:
my knowing of it will be the worst
of all deaths. It skips
sideways
from the path. I find
all foxes are gifts; afire, already skittering
away at your presence.

2

Exactness of the inexact
light on Moelwyn Fach;
dusty red-gold of an old
fox.

3

Every tale is a tale
of parting; the poet's
wife saw through
the kitchen window
a fox fleeing the hunt,

and opened a door
to it. It cooled its paws
in the slate-floored dairy
then left as it had come,
returned to its earth,
tail stiff, a brush
with death.

4

It pleased you most
to use the word *unruly*,
as you lifted my hair
again from your face,
and rose to make
the coffee.

5

After the Welsh of Williams Parry

Then with no
haste, no
fright, it slipped
its russet hide
over the ridge.
It happened:
the disturbance
of a shooting
star.

who, blind, saw

At nightfall, the things closest to us seem to move away from our eyes. So the visible world has moved away from my eyes, perhaps forever. JORGE LUIS BORGES

In the long midday of
Midsummer's Eve, three men
play catch with a pebble, as if they cast out
for their own shadows. Cardigan Bay is quiet.

Behind us, a blind man on the promenade taps
his cane on a lamp post. How can we know
one near thing from another?
You can watch it still:

Borges' lecture on blindness,
his hand curled on his thigh then
lifting for a moment. 'Yellow is still with me,
even now,' he says. It's in the bitter light

of the cataracted eye, but we can't keep it
from breaking. When we behead the yellow
flowers of St John's Wort, they give out
a red sap. Borges loved

yellow neckties, the caged
and rayed pelt of the tiger;

this hour, drawn out and through the air,
held briefly and released like a last line.

But there isn't a last, only this gradual
winding down. The arms tire, the eyes
tire. The blind man taps his cane
twice. Syllabic. Yellow.

the line trembles; mostly, when we would reel in the catch, there is nothing to see

I have been tormenting myself and the eels. SIGMUND FREUD

In 1876, at the Trieste zoological station
of Vienna's Institute of Comparative Anatomy,
a young Sigmund Freud dissected four hundred
eels in search of the gonads of the male
anguilla anguilla.
                    I take a walk
in the evening at 6.30, he wrote, my hands stained
from the white and red blood of the sea
animals and in front of my eyes the glimmering
debris of cells, which still disturb me
in my dreams...

I had a lover who would ask me, at times,
when my tongue slipped,
                what would Dr Freud say?
I hated it.
But, well, what would Herr Doktor
say? Of a young man of nineteen who closed
his eyes at night to see the slippery detritus of eelflesh,
the beheaded hundreds; his hands searching the deeps
in their bellies, feeling for what he knew
must be there but never finding it.

Four hundred?
            Sigmund, that's what you call flogging
            a dead horse.

It's true, we have never known
            where they come from.
If only he'd heard the stories of beginnings
– how some folk believed the eel
                    was born of strands loosed
from the tail of a horse,
        and fallen into water.

—

I'm sorry I thought I saw something
move beneath the skin of the river.

—

they originate in what are called the entrails of the earth, which are found spontaneously in mud or moist earth ARISTOTLE

This is how the eel is made.
We take a ribbon of albumen,
and infuse it with clear Sargasso
blood. Translucent, at first,
then marred to a darker
skin, it drifts until it makes river-

fall, where we change the eyes to gold
and leave it to feed and fatten
on bugs and crayfish and old flesh
rotting the riverbed. Here it learns
it is lonely. Also how to slip the hook,
and tooth quietly at the mud.

After years like this, we reignite
the blood, earth the wires
of its homing beacon. Salt rises, blues
the eyes, changes the skin. Called back
in a cold-finned dash, it swims to algal
arms, an offering to it who has none.

—

I'm sorry I thought I heard you
calling out to your sister.

—

After Montale

the eel's a twist of fire,
a tongue-lashing, love's barbed
arrow in the worn earth,

lonely, and brought back

only by gullies or a near dried-
out brook,

to a fertile haven;
deepgreen soul that's after
life, who seeks there –

where it will instead be bitten
by desolation, the driest thirst –
the spark that says everything

begins when everything
seems burnt back to charcoal,
a buried windpipe

—

I'm not sorry I still don't know
what Dr Freud would say.

—

Hammer the eel
to the wall, nail
through the head.
With a small
knife, cut a ring
around the throat.

You'll need a towel,
you aren't strong
in the hands.
Grasp the eel
at the neck, and
working its skin down,
peel it from the flesh.

about mountains it is useless to argue,

since they are silent, glacier-muffled, and
the light is upon them like a hand.

What can be said? The easterly wind
blows in from the feet of the dead,

rushes in and holds our words
to our tongues, draws the clouds

glowering down to the peak of Cnicht.
Above us, ravens dip their wingtips

to the current, turning with a deep
scull. Even in the mountains, haven't we

longed to be in the mountains? To unfold
on the surface like leprose lichen, or pull

at the roots of the mountain, or light
bonfires on the high ridges to drive

off the loose ends of winter. I have seen
some cross Crib Goch on hands and knees.

On the mountains we ask questions
with our bodies. Of how the oil-dark

tarns rest in high wallows – Lake of Stones
and Wethers, Dung Lake, the Llynau Cŵn,

Lakes of the Dogs. As we too could rest,
and no longer bicker – but the clefts

and corries were sluiced by glaciers
in a thousand-centuries hurry, and we

can't bear to think it, can't even watch
the clock hand ratchet through another minute.

an absence is how we become surer of what

It's the hour when gravity pulls on the
thigh-bones. It's not right to wake now,
but someone always does, stirred by a disturbance

of light that pales the stars. In Coed y Bleiddiau,
the old oak loses a leaf. A once-sleeping
woodpigeon shotguns through the clearing.

Let's say, then, this is where the last Welsh wolf
passed – burrs, seeds, the beginnings of mange,
in his coat; eyes yellowing into grief. Still, sure,

even winter dies off. But in his roaming, leaves
wet underfoot, something gripped him
into alertness. It woke me too. There will be
a last of everything.

On Ynys Enlli, the many saints were promised
that each would die in succession, in keeping
with his age, but even that blessing, in time,

wore away. Soon, another oak leaf will fail at
the stalk, and drift, dead-veined, to the rotting
ground of Coed y Bleiddiau. And here we will

try to build us a wolf of bent willow; pliable-
ribbed, taller even than a man; one who at last
feels nothing through the pads of its paws;

who scents not a thing. Not this first scatter of
rain, or the grey squirrel dashing in fear beneath
its hollow, wickered belly; nor everywhere
our lasting stench.

I was no tree walking

[*David Nash,* Wooden Boulder *(A Going Work), Maentwrog, 1978*]

I *From now on, the holy is fit for use*
then Hölderlin, wandering in
mind, lived
                    at last in Tübingen, high
above the river Neckar,
in the keep of a semi-literate carpenter.

Might madness
have smelt to him of sawn oak. Of the
swollen river, foam,
                    late death.

In my house, said the carpenter later, the poet saw
                    a drawing of a temple.
Make me one of wood, he begged me, knuckling the walls.
Don't be afraid, I said.

At times he scratched through offcuts, as if a word
were hidden
                    beneath. You can't always
plane your way back.   But then
what were all those words for.

Light's shavings, a cedar-curl.
The river moving on the ceiling.

Kinds of oblivion *in which not the faintest gleam of a star, not even*
the phosphorescence of rotten wood,
can reach us

2

in the evenings the poet would whisper, *build me*
a temple, in the ears of all woodmen.
Even a temple that will tumble
            & descend

open to everything
woodlice decay
ice   the relentless   waters

3 *But   Lovely it is to unfold*
The soul and our
brief life
& when the sculptor had at last carved a boulder
from the base of a fallen oak, he rolled it
to a waterfall in Bronturnor Uchaf,
where it turned

the deepest, unextinguished blue
of a slate quarry in the rain;
where also it bloomed
with frost & roiled

the shallows & was wedged
after a time beneath the drover's bridge,
& un-wedged, & rode lines
of drift on the splintered

river Dwyryd, past the stone cast by Twrog
in anger; brushed the otter hunting
waters grey as beaten tin,
meandered with restless, dying eels,

caught with the salmon on the widening
sandbars, & rubbed itself free of memory;
& cured in the marshes, rocking on tides
that were temperaments,

& then, after a quarter century, shook
itself free of everything, and was somehow
lost. As if a prayer could be rolled downhill,
always going, no question
of arrival

4 *Near is* *And difficult to grasp*
all your life you reach
for something –
 call it poetry if you like –
but can't lay a hand on it

& find instead the ticking of a leaf in
the wind, the immutable

walls against the palm, a river, even one
silent
                    hour

& your body becomes a tuning fork,
picks up words, barely signalled
it's just the way it's

wading
they say green   *is the hardest colour*
                    so many people falling
                    like   *rain*
                    from the sky

& it never eases, the thought:
I just want to go home

5 *Said the sculptor*
not that it's lost, it's just
somewhere else.

6
the afternoon traffic rushes
all one way from Dolgellau to Penrhyndeudrath
& the wind rocks the reeds & the wind rifles
through the river & the boulder
doesn't move –

shouldering the sluice of the waters
& unrocked even when the wind explodes
its downdraft on the marshtide.

I stand in a mess
of grasses and debris
on the tideline. There will be a time
to wade out to it, river to knees, thighs,
groin & belly & chest & throat, & even
with the water over our heads, none of us
will be redeemed –

still, they say the deep world is as
clear as the surface one, only it asks
more of us: death; this languid
extinguishment
of gorselight and reeds, & of the brush
of clouds on the peaks
& of the ravens & the gulls &
all the bloody sheep; of the men fixing
somewhere a rail signal & the two swans
both untouching & inseparate

& of what persists above and below,
the taste of salt
the abiding of the thing

like an old tree lightened of the snow's weight

Think of the tree,
who, quiet, might

wait for the starlings
or the last of the red

squirrels, for something
to remind it of how to bear.

Who might not
mind, as much as we

believe, the borers
and scrapings,

the lover's knife, or
a woodpecker,

the weight of snow
on its leaf-empty branches.

As children we'd
take lightly

the stairs to a
grandfather

we thought asleep
and wake him with

a brass bell, while he hid
fully clothed beneath

the quilt, and carried
laughing the weight

of our small bodies
piled over his.

we have eaten the blackberries and spat out the seeds, but they lie glittering like the eyes of a man

In September 2003, Gwydion, son of the poet R.S. Thomas and painter Elsi Eldridge, begins to sort through the last effects of his parents' estate.

The skull of a hare.
Cheese box containing a puffin's
beak and a Winsor & Newton leaflet
on preventing moth damage
and mildew in paintbrushes.
Envelope containing snow
bunting feathers.

Envelope containing birth
& marriage certificates.
A copy of the will, of the deeds to 'Arfryn'.
Envelope (*L. Garvin, Honey Merchants*)
containing the scales of a grey
mullet

Envelope containing woodcock
feathers; a dead prawn; the skin
of an adder

in the brambles
shed like this year,

Another, with grass seeds.
Phials of chaffinch feathers, those
of a cuckoo.

like
this year
this

Postcards of Menai Bridge & Ynys Enlli,
the peak of Quinag, a slate-splitter

last of us working
the deep veins
now   what did
you say,
hunger?
no, this is a
mallet, the splitting
chisel

in Merioneth

Leaflet on Phostrogen, a sheet of dried
flowers from Bethlehem.

Label of a tin of herring fillets.
Photo of Grannie Eldridge.
Three drawings of a tree
One drawing of a man with a staff,
and gulls

Photo of Elsi.
Photo of a shelduck

always broke
in widening circles
no matter what
was sinkered

Income tax returns 1966–1989.
Envelope of bits of silver foil
from Aunt Ethel.

Address book (empty)

ran with a dark current

On the crossing to Ynys Enlli

To the starboard, bird-flecked cliffs –
kittiwakes who call out their own names,
gannets arrowing down through the surface.

I wonder what the fish knows before it is taken.
If there is a difference between captive and captivated.
Is it a question of grip? I wonder what those people know,

who call seaweed *tangle*. The sound deceives,
at times. From the slopes of Mynydd Enlli, you can't see
how the tide might race, skate you out into the open waters

or onto rocks. Monks who came here first ghosted
the currents in boats of ox-hide. They knew a deep keel is
more quickly grasped, and dragged. What's the difference,

I wonder now, between treacherous and treachery.
Is it a question of wanting? You think you could stay here
and lose the names of everything, even yourself – and the price

would be to find the deepest intimacy with something
you couldn't speak. Just lichens under hand. The mumbled
bee, the hushed sea, the seal's melancholic howl coursing

the channel. But you won't stay. The gannet has a skull
like a crash helmet, can plummet to the water head first
from ninety metres up, and not feel a thing. It's a question

of not asking questions. And why not, for once. We'll
likely have a good summer, says the skipper. You can tell,
when the kittiwake dares to nest so low in the cliffs.

trees are about you

I was far from
the root of things and
therefore quiet
of mind. Picking

holly, breaking stems
with gloved hands.
In each waxy leaf
the gleam of winter's

flattest days. So few
berries this year,
and all of them out
of reach. I'd climbed

a steep slope, and in
reaching leant my whole
weight against a birch.
It was only right

to put my ear to it,
as once I'd auscultated
the chest of a man
I tried to love; whose

blood would press
to the inner meniscus
of skin, and skim
away. I heard this

time no sap, just
the tree's own
chambering, a hum
of branch scraping

with another birch
in the rising wind.
Then, four clear
knocks. Who hid

inside? Or asked
to leave? Or wanted
to come in; to the hill,
the open air, my

simple ear? Who's there,
I might have said.
Or found some other
question. Are you at home

in there? Knock,
knock. I know

of a man who,
faced with ancient

handprints in Chauvet
Cave, saw not an imprint,
but that someone still
pushed firmly

from the other side.
But what then of
the drawn bison,
the stalking panther?

Do they prowl and
moan behind it all,
coming at us through
even this bark, resolute.

Who's there, I want
to say. There are no limits
anymore. Everything burns
and dissipates or

somehow roots in.
Joseph Priestley
felt his one death closing
in, no more than a high

whine in the tips of
of the trees. He said
goodbye, and covered
his eyes, that no one

should witness what
passed. In the end,
we always seem to
face a kind of shame.

I moved my head away
from the tree's inner murmur.

I have no name for today but itself

Animals come when their names are called. Just like human beings. LUDWIG WITTGENSTEIN

Five inches of snow on the high track above the River
Esk. My godson pitches snowballs at the snowpiles
balanced on the fence posts. And misses.
We walk to the old gunpowder mill, emptied of volatility.

We're talking somehow of Wittgenstein,
who'd have urged us into this valley. The better
snowballs are made without gloves – the hands' heat
seals with a neat crust. We work the method to perfection,

walking still, and now hardly speaking, when a deer breaks
through into the open path. There's barely enough time
to see the nerve-scrabble under its coat, an electric thing,
fleeing and fleet. We have no words to carry the startle

of that hoof sinking through the first scab of snow; to suggest
the odour of nothingness itself in the deep

stream below; no name for the way the ear-twitch holds in it
a belief in things un- or barely seen. Like God, I don't dare
say. Wittgenstein would have said, there are things
that cannot be expressed. And yet they show themselves.

At times the animals here steam in the cold. I might say now,
unscientifically, it's the result of a rising damp, sadness that fills
its own reservoirs, and needs to be released. Because we're none
of us so different, after all. Everything goes quiet,

someone says later, when you see a deer in the yard.
You notice the silence. It's like the aftermath of a call.

the stars are fixed, but the earth journeys by strange migrations towards the cold

The eve before
Christmas Eve,
just one more night
without name.

I step outside
with a pan of blackened
Cumberland sausages,
let them sizzle and

smoke in the open
air. Those are the Hunter
Stars, icy punctures,
quaking, though it is not

hard to see instead
a saucepan, wielded
overhead, ready
to strike down on

the southern horizon
and peen flat the hills
in the Borders. I hold
the skillet outstretched.

No sky holds like this.
But it descends, blinding.
The kitchen, when I turn
back, is still thick with

smoke clustering
the downlights, like
insensible insects,
rushing towards what

they need least. I have
woken here to frost
stiffening the grass,
to a tractor winding

the white hill with
a tail of sheep, the River
Esk dark in the valley.
In the end, won't

the cold win? Most of
space is space, and
the universe settles
just above absolute zero,

where molecules stop
moving. My hands grow

stiff. It will be a task to
break this fist, to return

to the air filled
with carbon, the old
earth burning back
to its beginning.

all those good words; and I outside them

There are only, everywhere, differences and traces of traces.

JACQUES DERRIDA

Back, then, to the whitewashed
cottage by the Afon Glaslyn.
My face pale in the train window.
Outside, the soaked earth.
Pools rested in the lowlands
and held the grey light, somehow
the source of it.

It had rained all week, the river
at the foot of the cottage
wider than ever.
I was the only one left. The last –
but the first to be astonished
by a blackbird at the back door.
No one had swept the leaves
that fell in autumn, cornered
to the doorstep by winds, and now,
in late winter, they were wet
and half-decomposed.

The blackbird tossed at them
with its yellow beak. No doubt,
there were all kinds of small life

in there. It was the rustle,
the diligent rustle, that brought
me to put my face to the pane
in the door.

What about that word,
diligence. It meant *love*, once.
Now it means *effort.*

I suppose it saw me, then.
There was something like outrage
in its yellow-rimmed eye. It made
a small yelping noise, the quiet
and quick mew of a new puppy,
lifted its tail, and made a two-
footed hop back through
the leaves.

Did the blackbird and I see
the same face? Pale and tired
and not at all diligent? Traces
you could have no pity for.
I'd thought of blackbirds as flocking birds.
Lines of them on telephone wires,
or the veering black concentration
of them in flight. Where was the flock?
Where was its dissimulation?
Without the disturbance

in the leaves, I could hear
the river murmur its increase.
In the afternoon, I swept
the leaves away.

I hid myself in the side of the mountain

Tall, tall, tall, tall, tall man / you bend so as not to dent the firmament. REBECCA LINDENBERG

1

A giant is nothing
more than
an awfully tall
man.

2

The giant Idris liked to lie
on the mountainside, under stars white hot
as the magnesium light in his
physics class,

though the stars
left no afterburn in the eye; experimented
with seeing the universe drift
below instead of

above; felt how gravity held
its sweet pull on his long back, and left its scar
in the tiny horizontal marks
either side of

his spine, lines
that marked how he grew much too fast;

gave himself finally to the study of
feeling small.

This was good
for a time, but it built in him a whelming
rage. Then he stood
and cast out

stone after
stone from the seat of his mountain –
taller he kept saying taller –
and when at last

he stopped he saw
he had made the deep earth and the high
earth and still whatever
had rushed his

hollow legs
and come howling out was unappeased
but he was out
of stones.

3

This is not a strange turn of
events. Everywhere we find

the tall men turning
to stones.

4 *Autumn, 1856*
Alfred Lord Tennyson's wife, Emily,
watched him disappear up
the ridge, into rain that came pouring on over Cader Idris
and then she waited

(I never saw
anything more awful
than that great veil of
rain drawn straight
over Cader Idris, pale
light at the lower edge)

and of course he came down again.

And anyway, awful is not the word
it once was. It was just that Emily
was awed by her husband's receding
back,

(as if death were
behind it)

or by the rain, this matter of departure into a lowering
edgelight

5 *Summer, 1828*

Still a student at Cambridge, Charles Darwin summered
near Barmouth, and would ascend Craig yr Aderyn –
and, seated there, shoot the rare seabirds nested below.

We'll never know if, from time to time, he drew
his sights instead on the mountain to the north,
astonished by the fall on its flanks of wingshot light.

6

The giant Idris tilted
his great head upwards, and said, take for
example the blue supergiant
stars – Rigel

in the Orion
constellation, for one – they live, if you
can say they live, always
on the edge

of disaster,
radiating all of what they are ferociously
out from the core
and casting

layer after layer
of themselves out, in stellar winds of six million

kilometres an hour,
you think you

can imagine it but
you can't. Our old sun will power down and fade
but the blue supergiants
are left to rip

themselves open,
there is nothing as magnificent as the way we
shatter, but do I
have to shatter?

7 *Autumn, 2001*
when does a mountain make sense?
when you wake on its wrecked
spine –
but on this mountain it is said you might
not wake at all or wake mad or, worse,
a poet

the wind galed so fiercely up the north
ridge I had to line the base of the tent with
stones
and try to sleep pressed against the ground

a cold prostrate prayer of a night but when
I woke
I woke
in fog

8

It takes so long to figure out what to fear,
and even then we get it wrong.
The giant lies.

9 *Winter, 2011*

The bare trees
by the Afon Glaslyn. The frosted
surface of its pools. Light breaks
over

the siltstone
of the threshold mountains.
When did we start to talk about
light like this?

As if it is something
cast about. We have seen so many
things break, but the light in fact
breaks unbroken.
A hand has opened

out of weariness of the fist
and let the light fall. It does its work
to break up

the clouds at rest
on Cader Idris. It breaks on the shallow
frost of the roadsides, on the thawing
backs of the sheep

that lie
like stones of the field.

Notes

All poems in *Homing* take their titles from lines by the Welsh poet R.S. Thomas.
All definitions come from the *Shorter Oxford English Dictionary*.

without catching a thing I was not far from the truth: For L.R. 'If I closed my eyes for a minute...' – Raymond Carver, 'Drinking while Driving'.

For the section, 'Night Reading in the Porongurups', I am indebted to Eduardo Galeano's *Mirrors: Stories of almost everyone* (trans.M. Fried). I am also, of course, indebted to L., who drove us almost 2000 km through the south-west of Western Australia in five days, and who, in fact, won an argument or two.

the bone the island: The letter from Able Seaman Millich, with its misspelt 'buggary', was encountered in Andrew and Sandra Rose's *Man overboard!: The HMAS Nizam Tragedy*.

word only becomes at last the word: 'Bluff Knoll was called *Pualaar Miial* (great many faced hill) by the local Aboriginal people...The peak is often covered with mists that curl around the mountain tops and float into the gullies. These constantly changing mists were believed to be the only visible form of a spirit called *Noatch* (meaning dead body or corpse), who had an evil reputation.' austhrutime.com/stirling_range.htm.

I have let her ashes down in me like an anchor: For Elsie May.

where to turn without turning to stone: With thanks to L.W.

not like me whose migrations are endless: 'During this storme certain great fowles' – Richard Hawkins, 1593.

'Now I am ready to tell how bodies are changed' – Ted Hughes, *Tales from Ovid.*

The fifth part to this poem offers a loose translation of the final lines of Baudelaire's renowned poem 'L'Albatros' ('The Albatross').

the true trade: 'When the Messiah comes and the world ends...' – Annie Dillard, *For The Time Being.*

it was I it ground: 'Ground, like sleep, forgets for a living' – Philip Gross, 'Fantasia on a Theme from IKEA'.

there are no handrails: 'And then, before the late supper, this pensiveness' – Rilke, *The Notebooks of Malte Laurids Brigge* (trans. S. Mitchell).

meadows empty of him, animal eyes, impersonal as glass: 'to be a part of the outward life, to be out there at the edge of things' – J.A. Baker, *The Peregrine.*

The incident of the 'poet's wife' comes from the diaries of Mildred (Elsi) Eldridge, wife of R.S. Thomas. 'One morning there was a group of farmers pounding through the fields after a fox. I happened to look out the kitchen window which looked down the path to the river and there was the fox coming up the path, men and dogs about to cross the river. Quickly I opened the kitchen door and stood behind it, the fox came in, and I shut and locked the door. The fox went through the slate-floored dairy and stayed quietly, while men and dogs hullabalooed outside. Eventually they decided it had cut across the garden and they moved off. After a while I opened the door and left the fox to find its way back across the river.' See Byron Rogers, *The man who went into the west: the life of R.S. Thomas.*

The final part of the poem is inspired by the last lines of Robert Williams Parry's poem 'Y Llwynog' ('The Fox').

the line trembles; mostly, when we would reel in the catch, there is nothing to see: Richard Schweid's book, *Eel*, provided me with much of the inspiration and fascinating source material for this poem. I am indebted in particular to his description of how one might skin an eel.

This poem contains an inexact translation of some lines from Eugenio Montale's poem 'L'anguilla' ('The Eel'). My translation owes much to the ideas found in Paul Muldoon's chapter on 'The Eel' in his book *The End of the Poem.*

I was no tree walking: I have taken the account of Hölderlin's madness from Michael Hamburger's introduction to Hölderlin's *Selected Poems and Fragments*. 'In one of his periodic letters to Hölderlin's mother – who seems never to have visited her son in all the years up to her death in 1828 – the semi-literate carpenter informs her…'His poetic spirit still shows itself to be active, for instance in my house he saw the drawing of a temple. He told me to make one out of wood. I replied that I have to work for my living, that I am not so fortunate as to live in philosophic calm like him, immediately he replied, "Oh, I am a wretched creature"…' *Selected poems and fragments*, trans. M. Hamburger (London: Penguin Books, 1998), p.xxxvi.

The epigraphs throughout are from Hölderlin's poems. The line 'the deep world is as clear as the surface one...' is by Jose Ortega y Gasset, from *Meditations of Quixote* (1914).

I am also indebted to David Nash's own notes and descriptions of the lifespan of his extraordinary art piece *Wooden Boulder*. See *David Nash* (London: Thames & Hudson, 2007).

I have no name for today but itself: For Hamish and Naomi.

all those good words; and I outside them: 'There are only, everywhere, differences' – Jacques Derrida, *Positions*, trans A. Bass (Chicago, University of Chicago Press, 1982).

I hid myself in the side of the mountain: The account of Tennyson's visit to Cader Idris can be found in: C.Y. Lang and E.F. Shannon eds., *The letters of Alfred Lord Tennyson: 1851–1870* (Cambridge, MA: Harvard University Press, 1987), p.158.

The Giramondo Publishing Company acknowledges the support of Western Sydney University in the implementation of its book publishing program.

This project has been assisted by the Commonwealth Government through the Australia Council, its arts funding and advisory body.